Using Facebook Groups For Your Family History & Genealogy

MELISSA DICKERSON,
GENEALOGY GIRL TALKS

This book is dedicated to all the family and friends I've met using Facebook Groups for my own family history and genealogy.

CONTENTS

ACKNOWLEDGMENTS

I wish to personally thank the following people for the contributions to my inspiration and other help in creating this book:

You know who you are! Every person who I have shared my dreams with and who has showed interest in helping me pursue my dreams, thank you! Your kindness and encouragement has pushed me forward. I could never repay each of you. Perhaps, a simple "Thank you!" will suffice.

1 WHAT ARE FACEBOOK GROUPS?

According to Facebook's Help page, Facebook Groups are defined as this, "Facebook Groups make it easy to connect with specific sets of people, like family, teammates or coworkers. Groups are dedicated spaces where you can share updates, photos or documents and message other group members. You can also select one of three privacy options for each group you create."

We are all familiar with Facebook and its many benefits in the social realm, but did you know Facebook can also assist you in your Genealogy and Family History research?

These "dedicated spaces" are helpful if you know how to use them. This guide, **"Using Facebook Groups for Genealogy"** will give you basic concepts related to the use of Facebook Groups for your Genealogy and Family History research.

How you use the groups, and your level of participation, will determine your results. Some groups are more active than others. Some have many members while others have few.

Now that you know what Facebook Groups are, let's get started on how to use them for your own family research.

2 TYPES OF FACEBOOK GROUPS

Before I explain how to access Facebook's Groups, I would like to explain the different types of groups found on Facebook. While this is not an all inclusive list of Facebook Group types, it does contain the general types available.

Keep in mind, if you don't find a Group you are interested in, you can always create your own!

7 Types of Facebook Groups:

1. General Genealogy Groups.

These groups mainly focus on research and related questions of a broad nature. For example, you can ask general questions related to record locations, research help, share your findings, and help others. Don't overlook these General Genealogy Groups. There are a lot of helpful and knowledgable people in these groups!

2. Location Specific Groups.

These groups are my personal favorite. These groups can focus on research at the region, state, or even the county level. If you are fortunate, you will find a local historian/ author who specializes in the area your ancestors lived.

You can post questions about your family's history, the history of the location you are researching, connect with others, and, don't forget, help others in their research.

3. Surname Groups.

Surname Groups are predominantly based on a family surname. When you are looking for common surnames, be sure to check the location. Some Facebook Groups combine surnames and locations to help other researchers find them.

There are many Gibson Family researchers, for example, but you may only be interested in the Gibson Family from Virginia. Be sure to check the location, if available, for the Surname Groups.

4. Society/Organization Groups.

These Groups can be helpful if your ancestors were members of organizations. They can also help you if you, as a researcher, are a member of Historical Societies, Genealogical Societies, or other organizations.

5. Genetic Genealogy Groups.

These Groups can be both broad Groups and surname specific Groups. With the rising interest in DNA and

Genetic Genealogy these groups are very popular. Once again, you will find helpful and knowledgable people in these groups.

6. Family Groups.

Many families will create their own group to connect with other family members. These types of groups are helpful when you are researching the same family. Combining your research with others is a great way to learn more!

7. Ethnicity Related Groups.

These Groups are helpful if you are researching, for example, German Genealogy and need assistance. Some members will even translate documents to assist others.

There are many different types of Facebook Groups that will help you in your Family History research. Some of these Groups combine several types. For example, there are Surname Groups specific to certain locations. When you are searching for Facebook Groups to join, consider combining the location and/or surname in your search.

3 HOW TO ACCESS FACEBOOK GROUPS

Facebook Groups are easy to access on both your mobile device and computer. You can visit Facebook at www.facebook.com. If you are using an Android or Apple phone, you can access the Facebook app the same way you would access other apps you download.

Once you have the app installed, or open the website on your computer, you need to sign in. If you don't have a Facebook account, you will need to create one prior to visiting and joining Facebook's Groups.

I will first walk you through accessing Facebook Groups on your mobile app. At the top of the screen you will see a search bar. Some devices show the actual word "Search" in a white font. Click on this bar and add your search terms. Some examples of search terms to use are: "Lincoln County NE Genealogy," "Gibson Family Research," "Melungeon," "Lee County Virginia," "German Genealogy," and "Jones DNA Study."

After you enter the search terms, press the enter button. A

list of results will be displayed. Keep in mind that you are looking for Groups to follow. On Apple devices there is a scrolling bar at the top of the screen that allows you to narrow your results to display only Facebook's Groups. Click on this and you will see a list of Groups to choose from.

Once you select the Group you would like to learn more about, click it and you will arrive at the Group's page. From here you can navigate around the Facebook Group, join the Group, view a description of the Group, and more.

There are a few key points to know if you are new to Facebook's Groups:

Facebook Groups can be either public or closed.

A public Group is a Group that anyone, anywhere can access. A closed Group is one that is more private. In a closed Group, your posts are not public to anyone, anywhere, but they can be seen by all the members within the Group.

Closed Groups will require you to join them.

If a Group is set to "closed" by the administrator, you will need to send a request to join the Group. The time it takes for your request to be accepted or denied depends on the availability of the administrators.

Most Public Groups allow you to join immediately.

If a Group is set to "public" you can choose to either join the Group or not. You are able to view public Group content, but, if you choose to join the Group, you will see posts and information in your newsfeed.

View the Groups information and description.

Viewing the Group's information and description will help you determine if the Group is a good fit for you and your research.

Familiarize yourself with the Group administrators.

It is always a good idea to familiarize yourself with the Group's administrators. These are the individuals who will help you if an issue arises within the Group.

Review rules and policies.

Many Facebook Groups have rules and policies regarding posting, soliciting, and general conduct within the Group. Become familiar with these policies.

Facebook Groups are a valuable tool in Family History and Genealogy research. The more familiar you become with them (and the flow of the Groups you choose to join) the more rewarding your experience will be.

4 YOUR PRIVACY & FACEBOOK GROUPS

Now you know what Facebook Groups are, the different types of Groups, how to access them, and a few key points to using them. Now, let's focus our attention on your privacy and your use of Facebook Groups.

Some individuals are open with sharing their information with others and some individuals are more reserved. The decision to share your information is personal preference. Only you can decide the extent of information you will share.

My suggestion is to be broad with your details. I personally share information about ancestors a few generations back, but only those who are deceased. I suggest not sharing information about living relatives. I also suggest keeping information regarding your parents and children private - I don't share this information either.

Only you can determine the level of personal information you share. You are responsible for keeping your personal, private information safe.

As you pursue the use of Facebook Groups, be sure to act responsibly.

5 GET THE MOST OUT OF FACEBOOK GROUPS

I will approach this chapter from a research perspective. If you are joining Facebook Groups to connect with family and cousins, your experience may be different than someone who is interested in Facebook Groups for research.

The first point to remember when joining Facebook Groups is to interact! You will get the most out of your experience by interacting, helping others, offering advice, commenting on posts, adding posts, and liking others' posts. Don't just take information, but continue to offer information. Get in there and mingle!

As stated above an important part of getting the most out of your experience is by interacting. One way to interact is to write a post in the Group. Before you write your post, be sure to review and follow the policies and rules for posting within the Group. Each Group has their own rules and policies.

You may be wondering what to include in your post.

Generally, that will depend on the information you are seeking. If you are looking for family to connect with, be sure to include your ancestor's date of birth, date of death, location, and any other information that will assist others in helping you. Try to add as much information as you can so others can help. If you are looking for general information about a location, ask for that information. For example, if you are looking for the name of an area, a rural road, or, perhaps, the name of a building in a specific location, then give specific information in your post. Be clear with your question.

I've found in my own experiences with using Facebook Groups that interaction is the most important part of any Group. The most active Groups (those with a lot of participation) are the most fun and helpful Groups to join.

6 START YOUR OWN FACEBOOK GROUP

If your search for a Facebook Group to meet the needs of your research have not been successful, you can start your own Facebook Group. Starting your own Group is fairly simple. You just need to plan ahead and give it a good name.

Planning Ahead

1. The first thing to consider when starting your own Facebook Group is the name of the Group. You want to choose a name that will allow others to easily find your Group using Facebook's search feature. Consider adding locations and names to your Facebook Group's Name.

2. You will also want to consider whether your Group will be public (anyone can see it and anyone can join), closed (anyone can see the Group, but only members can see the posts within the Group), or secret (only seen by those who are members).

3. Plan out your Group's description and policies before you start your Group. What type of posts will you allow from your members? Who can post within the Group? What is the main focus of your Group? These are questions to consider when setting up your Group.

4. You will also want to add a cover image (the image at the top of your Group's page) to your Group. Select an image that applies to your Group's focus and is appealing to your members.

5. Consider how you will add members to your Group. Will you allow others to add members themselves? Are administrators the only individuals who can add members? Who will approve membership to your Facebook Group?

Once you have an idea of the focus of your Facebook Group, you are ready to create it!

Follow the steps below to successfully create your Facebook Group:

1. At the top of your Facebook page there is a link that states "Create Group." Click on that link.
2. Name your Facebook Group.
3. Add new members to your Group.
4. Select your privacy settings.
5. Add your cover image.
6. Add your Groups's description.

You are ready to let others know about your group! Be sure to keep up to date on your group, comment on posts, review posts from others, and to keep it interactive.

7 WHY USE FACEBOOK GROUPS?

I've been using Facebook Groups for a few years now and I love them! I can contribute a lot of my success (in my own Genealogy and Family History research) to the results I've had in the Groups I've joined. I am a member of several Surname related Groups, a few Ethnic related Groups, and some Location based Groups. I've learned so much from the individuals in these Groups, made connections with new cousins, researched "sideways" (my ancestor's siblings), and made a lot of progress.

I would like to share a few of the successes I've had using Facebook Groups.

I created a Facebook Group for one of my family surnames a few months ago. While the member numbers are low, the participation is high. I created this Group due to the fact that my uncle and I continually ran into people (in other groups) who were researching the same family surname that we were researching. This line caused brick walls for them the same way it was causing brick walls in our research.

It seemed the best way to get pass this brick wall was to create a place where we could discuss and compare our research. That is what we do! Someone will post their information, we discuss it, and we try to answer the burning question of "who are the parents of this elusive ancestor?"

I am also a member of a Location Based Facebook Group for both of my parent's families. My parents both have roots in the same county in West Virginia. My maternal Grandparents moved to Northeast Ohio when my mother was young. My paternal Grandparents stayed in the same county, but my father moved to Northeast Ohio in his early twenties. That is where he met my mother. Since they both have roots in the same county, I began looking for a group for that county. Boy, did I hit the jackpot with that group!

I've made more family connections than I can count and met some amazing people! Maybe you'll get lucky and meet an author and historian local to the county your family is from, too!

There is a group of individuals known as the Melungeons. If you are familiar with Appalachian research you may have come across this word a few times. I came across this in my own family research and became very intrigued since it seemed I had a connection to them. I scoured the internet, years ago, looking for more information. Somehow, I came across a Facebook Group and joined.

Now, while looking back, that has been one of my best decisions in this journey! Once again, I've met some amazing people in that group, too. There are members with a lot more information than I have and members that are just beginning to learn about these people. We all share and help each other. It's a very active Group and I can't thank these members enough for all the knowledge I've gained from them.

These are just a few examples of the success I've had using Facebook Groups. I hope they inspire you to join a few or, at the very least, cause you to consider using them for your own Genealogy & Family History.

8 GET OUT THERE AND GET STARTED!

I hope I've inspired you to get started with Facebook's Groups! They are a great resource and, best of all, they are FREE! Anyone with a Facebook account can access them.

So, what are you waiting for?

Get out there and get started **"Using Facebook Groups For Genealogy"** today!

If you've had success with Facebook Groups in your journey, I would love to hear from you!

You can find me on Twitter, Facebook, Pinterest, and Instagram. Just search for "Genealogy Girl Talks" and you'll find me. You can also send an email to genealogygirltalks@gmail.com

ABOUT THE AUTHOR

 Melissa Dickerson, also known as "Genealogy Girl Talks" has been conducting family history and genealogy research for over twenty years. She has a love of history, family, teaching, and creativity. Those four passions pushed her to create Genealogy Girl Talks in 2014.

She wrote her first eBook, "10 Tips for Using Pinterest for Family History" in the Fall 2014. That was followed by several more quick tip eBooks. In May 2016, her first print book was self-published ("Using Pinterest for Family History and Genealogy").

Melissa lives in Northeast Ohio, but her roots find her deep in pursuit of her family history in Appalachia. Her burning desire to learn more about her family and her roots in Southwestern West Virginia has quickly become her life's pursuit.